DON'T CALL ME "BEV"!

Things That Work My Last Nerve

DON'T CALL ME "BEV"!

Things That Work My Last Nerve

By
Beverly D. Washington

TRAFFORD PUBLISHING
6E–2333 Government St.
Victoria, BC CANADA
v8t-4p4

© Copyright 2005 Beverly D. Washington.
All rights reserved. No part of this publication may be reproduced, stored in a retrieval system, or transmitted, in any form or by any means, electronic, mechanical, photocopying, recording, or otherwise, without the written prior permission of the author.

Note for Librarians: A cataloguing record for this book is available from Library and Archives Canada at www.collectionscanada.ca/amicus/index-e.html
ISBN 1-4120-7210-7

Printed on paper with minimum 30% recycled fibre. Trafford's print shop runs on "green energy" from solar, wind and other environmentally-friendly power sources.

Offices in Canada, USA, Ireland and UK

This book was published *on-demand* in cooperation with Trafford Publishing. On-demand publishing is a unique process and service of making a book available for retail sale to the public taking advantage of on-demand manufacturing and Internet marketing. On-demand publishing includes promotions, retail sales, manufacturing, order fulfilment, accounting and collecting royalties on behalf of the author.

Book sales for North America and international:
Trafford Publishing, 6E–2333 Government St.,
Victoria, BC v8t 4p4 CANADA
phone 250 383 6864 (toll-free 1 888 232 4444)
fax 250 383 6804; email to orders@trafford.com

Book sales in Europe:
Trafford Publishing (UK) Limited, 9 Park End Street, 2nd Floor
Oxford, UK ox1 1hh UNITED KINGDOM
phone 44 (0)1865 722 113 (local rate 0845 230 9601)
facsimile 44 (0)1865 722 868; info.uk@trafford.com

Order online at:
trafford.com/05-2105

10 9 8 7 6 5 4 3 2 1

Table of Contents

Why I Wrote This Book ix

Acknowledgments xi

Chapter 1—Personal Things 1

    Shortcutters: People Who Abbreviate Your Name 3

    Time Stealers: People Who Are Always Late 5

    Ear Busters: People Who Speak at One Volume...LOUD! 9

    Intruders: People Who Invade Your Personal Space 11

    Bumpers: People Who Don't Apologize When They Bump Into You ... 13

Chapter 2—Workplace Things 15

    Baggage Carriers: People Who Bring Their Personal Problems to Work 17

    Responsenayers: People Who Don't Respond to Their Messages ... 19

    Delayers: People Who Don't Get Back to You 21

    Snatchers: People Who Take Things Without Your Permission 23

    Overcommitters: People Who Don't Fulfill Their Commitments ... 25

    Cell Phone Junkies: People Who Yak on Their Cellular Phones .. 27

Chapter 3—Bathroom Things 31

Germ Carriers: People Who Don't Wash After Using the
Bathroom 33

Messy Wipers: People Who Splash Water on the Sink and Don't
Wipe It Up 35

Naked Toilets: Companies That Don't Supply Toilet Seat
Protectors 37

Chapter 4—Picking and Scratching Things 41

Grazers: People Who Eat from Open Bulk Food Containers 43

Twirlers: People Who Play with Their Hair Around Open Food
Bars 45

Nose Pickers: People Who Pick Their Nose in Public Places 47

Privates Scratchers: Men Who Scratch Their Crotch in Public 49

Chapter 5—Food Things 51

Tongue Scoopers: People Who Use Their Tongue for Scooping
Food 53

Wide Mouths: People Who Talk with Their Mouth Full 55

Noisy Mouths: People Who Eat, Drink, and Smack on the
Telephone 57

Gum Crackers: People Who Chew Gum Loudly and Pop It
Incessantly 59

Ice Crunchers: People Who Chew Ice in Public 61

Teeth Suckers: People Who Suck Their Teeth After Eating 63

Nose Blowers: People Who Use Dinner Napkins To Blow Their
Nose 65

Chapter 6—Street Things 67

Spitters: People Who Spit on Sidewalks...69

Blindsiders: People Who Don't Look Before Exiting a Room or Building... 71

Weave Walkers: People Who Weave as They Walk Down the Street 73

Hoggers: People Who Walk Shoulder to Shoulder on the Sidewalk..75

Puffers: People Who Smoke in Front of Building Entrances.................77

Roadblockers: People Who Stand in the Middle of Corridors and Aisles 79

Chapter 7—Surprise Things................................. 81

Clueless: People Who Give Thoughtless Gifts.....................................83

Cheap Tippers: People Who Don't Tip Appropriately 85

Surprisers: People Who Bring Uninvited Guests to a Party 87

Cheapskates: People Who Don't Pay Their Fair Share When Dining Out 89

Slim Stickers: People Who Drink with the Stirrer Still in the Glass 91

Chapter 8—Retail Sales Things.......................... 93

Chit-Chatters: Salespeople Who Socialize with Others While Waiting on You 95

Unprofessionals: Salespeople Who Argue with Their Customers.......97

Chapter 9—Movie Things 99

Story Blockers: People Who Want To Tell You the Plot of a Movie 101

Interrupters: People Who Talk During Films 103

Reactors: People Who Talk at the Movie Screen 105

Chapter 10—Travel Things 107

Aisle Hoggers: People Who Pull Oversized Luggage Down Airplane Aisles 109

Space Stealers: People Who Put Their Luggage Underneath Their Seats 111

Seat Tuggers: People Who Tug and Lean on Your Seatback 113

Chapter 11—Hotel Things 115

Room Doom: Hotel Rooms That Have Not Been Properly Cleaned 117

Half-Views: Hotels That Lack Full-length Mirrors in the Guest Rooms 119

Inconsiderates: Guests Who Carry on Loud Conversations in the Hallways 121

Chapter 12—Other Things 123

Advantage Takers: People Who Try To Take Advantage of You 125

Insinceres: People Who Don't Keep Their Word 127

Excuse Makers: People Who Make Excuses for Anything and Everything 129

Why I Wrote This Book

Boy, oh, boy. At times, people work my last nerve. Certain things happen that cause me to ask, "Are people just not paying attention?"

Case in point. Whenever I introduce myself, I very slowly and deliberately say: *Beverly Washington*. Not too difficult. Very American. Very easy to remember.

Or so I thought! Would you believe that people still have the audacity to call me "BEV"? What nerve!

Maybe, you, too, have had it happen to you. Well, I am fed up with it, and that's why I've written this book. I wanted to address, very openly, all of the annoying things people do that get on my nerves and maybe yours, too! It's about time to set them straight. And if by doing so it causes some people to get upset...well, so be it. It's time they knew that abbreviating or changing my name is not permitted!

I want those who read this book to understand that many of the annoying things boil down to just plain rudeness. Have you ever been in situations in which the people you work with are unprofessional? Unethical? Rude? Unreliable? Well, I experience it often in business. So I was motivated to put pen to paper and write about the people who just don't get it: those who lack professionalism and the social graces.

Gentle readers, not only have I pointed out these offenses, I have provided you with survival tips designed to help you navigate through life as you tolerate these rude people. Feel free to use these tips. By doing so, you will keep your stress level down and maybe increase theirs. Hmm.

So enjoy the read. If you have other things that work your last nerve and would like to see them in print, please e-mail me at factorbw1@aol.com.

Remember...it's **Beverly,** not Bev!

Acknowledgments

I would like to acknowledge the following people for assisting me in the creation of this book: Sue Wasylik for being my mentor throughout this project; Angela Higginbotham for taking the time to review the initial draft; Dyahanne Ware, whose words of inspiration and enthusiasm kept me focused; Tina Jenkins Bell for referring me to my editorial wizard, Mark Boone; Hallie Belt, for being my Proofreading Princess; and Ken Smith for the wonderful illustrations. And, of course, my family, whose love I cherish. I am blessed.

Chapter 1

Personal Things

Shortcutters

People Who Abbreviate Your Name

A person's name is his or her most personal and important means of identification. We are branded by it from birth.

As a young child, I remember having to learn to respond to it, to pronounce it, to spell it, and to write it—starting with trying to place the letters, with perfection, on ruled notebook paper. As a child in school learning to write, I would attempt to write my name all sorts of different ways: Fancy, plain, block letters, italic...you name it, I tried it. *Beverly*. Three syllables. Writing the name with a huge "B." I even remember my childhood friends having difficulty pronouncing my name. They added a second "B" in place of the "V" and called me *Beberly*. That was okay. Funny, the things we remember from our childhood!

What I also remember is that no one ever shortened my name by calling me "Bev"!

It wasn't until I entered college that people started calling me "Bev". I suppose they wanted to sound friendlier, more familiar with me. Or maybe it was because whenever my name appeared in the newspaper, it was written as *Bev Washington*. So, in college, "Bev" was what I was called.

So what's everyone's excuse now? I always introduce myself as "Beverly." Formal, elegant, and ME! I even take pride in writing my name. As I script it, it starts out with a HUGE "B," allowing other letters to fall in line in a fluid design...*Beverly*. Now, I've been called other (some less complimentary) names that start with the letter "B"; however, they don't bother me as much as "Bev"!

Survival Tip:

* Never allow others to alter your name without your permission.
* Politely correct them. It's your name, and it's your choice whether people pronounce it correctly. Your name is part of your identity. Protect it. Love it. It's a precious commodity that belongs to you.

Time Stealers

People Who Are Always Late

They arrive late to work...they're tardy for meetings...and they always complete their assignments after the deadline. And, of course, they have valid excuses. At least, valid in their minds.

The people who are always pulling this late thing are the very people I refuse to plan anything with because I know they won't be on time! You know who I'm referring to.

Some of you reading this chapter may think that I'm being a bit too serious about this. Yes, I am! Late is late is late! If I put out the effort to be on time, doggone it, other people can, too! Okay, let me take a break. I realize that situations happen.

Emergencies occur, but come on, folks, not every day. Being on time is about showing respect and valuing the time and effort others put into being on schedule. It's about being responsible, isn't it? Interestingly, the very people who are always late are the first to be critical of others who run behind schedule. Figure that one out.

Survival Tip:

* **Work-related Survival Tip**
Make a point to send out reminders when things are due—especially at the office, where others are involved.

If you are the manager, check in with the staff at scheduled times to assess the progress of an employee's work. Ask for a rough draft or an outline to be submitted before the employee begins an assignment. It will help the person meet the deadline.

* **Relationship Survival Tip**
If it's a friend who runs late, make a reminder phone call and tell him or her that you have other commitments during the day, so it is imperative that he or she meet you at the scheduled time. Exchange telephone numbers and give the telephone number of the location should the person need to call. I recommend the customary wait time of fifteen minutes. After that, it's time to move on. It's important to bring the lateness issue to the surface so your friends become aware of how tardiness can negatively affect the relationship. Solicit their suggestions to help remedy the problem. Hey, I know: people are only human.

Allow me to share a short story with you. I remember dating a guy (for a short time, mind you) who was always late. It was annoying always having to wait for him to pick me up. I tried patience, and when that wore thin, I started plotting. I'd give him an earlier time to pick me up just to get him on his way in a timely manner. That worked for awhile until he caught on. Then I figured out that being late was a part of his personality. My response? Good-bye! Well, there were other things, too, that contributed to the split, but the lateness was a biggie!

* **Deadline Survival Tip**

Everyone has missed at least one deadline and probably paid the price for it. However, there are those who are always missing deadlines. What's their problem? Have they forgotten that other people are important, too? They have to remember that they're being counted on. They've made a commitment. It's time that they get their act together. Here are my suggestions for coping with colleagues' tardiness.

Should you continue to experience someone else's tardiness, point out the effect it's having on you. Then, make a decision as to how long you're going to tolerate it. Seek the person's help in maintaining a healthy relationship, but hang tough. Remember: it's going to take him time to get it.

BEVERLY D. WASHINGTON

Ear Busters

People Who Speak at One Volume...LOUD!

Have you ever had a conversation with someone who talks LOUD and doesn't even realize it? On the phone, in person—it doesn't matter...LOUD, LOUD, LOUD! Okay, we can all get a little loud sometimes—even Beverly—but not *all* of the time. It's frustrating at times, especially when quieter volumes are the preferred levels...as in public places.

I know a postal clerk who talks extremely loudly when assisting customers. His voice carries across the entire room. Because of his volume, I make a huge effort to avoid him if he's the next available clerk. It's unfortunate. He's oblivious to the whole thing. I know another person who talks loudly. Perhaps he has a hearing defect. I don't know. Maybe it's this person's need to be heard.

Oh, I'll have to admit that there are times when I've been overcome with excitement and expressed myself too loudly. I've even laughed a bit too excitedly. However, I've immediately apologized and regained control. It is out of respect for others that I do so.

Survival Tip:

If you are with someone who talks too loudly, simply lower your volume. He or she may sense something is wrong and follow your lead. Or, be honest, and say, "Let's keep our voices low so as not to disturb others." If you can, take the conversation to another place where no one else is around. Somewhere out in the wilderness might be a good idea.☺

Intruders

People Who Invade Your Personal Space

You have my attention! Your touching, tapping, or poking is not necessary. People can get so wrapped up in their conversations that, in order to assure them you are paying attention, they feel the need to touch. What's that all about? Are they missing the fact that you are giving them eye-to-eye contact and all of the other necessary communication signals?

More than once I've walked away from a conversation with my arm bruised. People and their behaviors! Who can figure them out? I'll admit it. I have a few idiosyncrasies myself, but one thing I can say is that I work very hard not to bring injury to other people when I'm talking to them.

Survival Tip:

If you know someone who is a poker, tapper, or toucher, you may want to:

* Gently make him aware of his behavior. He may be unaware of his actions.
* Point out that many people are offended when being touched without their permission.
* Inform him that touching outside of the customary handshake is inappropriate in the business environment and may lead to unwanted, negative perceptions.
* Use subtle humor. *OUCH!* Or, *"You shocked me again with your touching!"* (Subtlety is not my strongest virtue.)
* Warning: Avoid poking back in retaliation. This may create other problems.☺

Bumpers

People Who Don't Apologize When
They Bump Into You

It takes only two little words: "Excuse me." How difficult can it be to remember to say them? When someone bumps into you, "Excuse me" should follow. I am sure the person felt the nudge, too. I know: people can be in their own little world sometimes. Or, perhaps they may not feel that saying "excuse me" is necessary, but as an expression of common courtesy, it is.

Survival Tip:

Should someone accidentally bump into you, just say to him or her (only if the person appears normal), "Oh, you just bumped into me, or did we just collide?" At that point, the person would say, "Excuse me" or "I'm sorry"—if he or she is normal. Should an individual bump into you who does not appear to be normal, just keep walking. As a matter of fact, put some pep in your step. Getting into a confrontation may prove to be unhealthy for you. Not everyone who *appears* normal *is* normal.☹

Chapter 2

Workplace Things

Baggage Carriers

People Who Bring Their Personal Problems to Work

There should be a rule for how much time people are allowed to discuss their personal problems at work. I realize that the work environment must allow for personal exchange and interaction, but not *all* day, *every day*—especially when there is work to be done. Still, some people just don't get it. They bring their personal problems to work and talk about what's not going right in their life...all day long. Ultimately, this negativity affects their job performance, leading to unproductive behaviors.

Survival Tip:

* Should you be the one who's affected by such people, suggest that they save the discussions for their break, lunch, or (better yet) after work. Suggest that focusing on their work may increase their productivity, creating a stronger feeling of control and accomplishment.
* If you are a very good friend to a person who brings her personal problems to the office, perhaps suggest to her that she seek professional help. This suggestion protects your own mental health and well-being and prevents a drop in your own productivity.

Responsenayers

People Who Don't Respond to Their Messages

With all of the wonderful new technology available, people still can't seem to use it effectively. What's wrong with people these days? You call someone, you leave a message at his or her request, and the person still forgets to return your call. I'm not advocating that you return every message you receive (solicitors can be ignored!). I am referring to people you know and work with. It only takes a few minutes to get back to someone.

Gentle readers, just return the call! Answer the question! And, if you prefer that no further dialogue is needed, just say so. Be considerate...don't keep people guessing! Let the person know if there's a better time to contact you. It's just that simple.

Survival Tip:

Leave a second message indicating the details of the initial call. Politely say in your message that you have been waiting for a response. Firmly state that you are willing to proceed to the next step by a specific date. Leave your telephone number again, in case the person has misplaced it. Then move to Plan B.

Delayers

People Who Don't Get Back to You

You've been asked to write a proposal for a new business consideration. They want you to get moving on it immediately. They say they're interested in doing business with you, so you bust your buns and get it done. You submit it. And then you wait. And wait. And wait. And no one gets back to you. What's going on? You say, "I thought it was a high priority!" You then get on the phone and leave message after message. Still no response. No one bothers to get back to you. This is drama! Unnecessary drama at that!

People will have you jumping through hoops if you allow them to. Everyone is busy, so why not just keep people informed? Say, "I'm not interested" or "We've found someone else." It's common courtesy.

Survival Tip:

Prepare yourself. You can't change people. Those who refuse to follow up will probably not make it a priority unless you attach a consequence to their behavior. So do it. Make it worth their time to follow up with you. This may help decrease your worry time. Some other helpful hints:

* Verbally confirm a date when they are expected to get back to you.
* Send a follow-up letter confirming that date.
* Make a call asking for an update, a decision, or a next step.
* If no decision is given at that time, suggest another follow-up date, putting them on notice that you will call back.
* Make the call.
* Close with a follow-up letter expressing your continued interest, saying that you look forward to hearing from them at their convenience.
* Now it's time to move on.

Call a favorite client just to hear how things are going. This is a good-news, ego-building call that will do wonders to improve your mood and provide new inspiration to help you move forward, releasing your feeling of being stuck and helpless.

Snatchers

People Who Take Things Without Your Permission

I don't know about you, but I feel very uncomfortable taking something from someone else's desk and not returning it. We all get busy at times and we forget, but we should all remember to return another person's property. Always. Going into someone's office and taking things is an untrustworthy act. People should be able to leave work, home, or anywhere else without having to concern themselves about whether their personal property will be there upon their return. Show respect for the property of others both at home and at the office. Remember, if it's not yours, don't touch it!

Survival Tip:

For those of you who are trusting of others, err on the side of caution by leaving all valuables in a secure place under lock and key.

Overcommitters

People Who Don't Fulfill Their Commitments

Gentle readers, several of you would no doubt agree that volunteering is a wonderful thing. When we get involved, it's because we want to give our time to help others. But how about the people who put their names on the line to help out and are nowhere to be found when the work begins or are always too busy to make the meetings or take charge of an assignment? My question to them is, "Why did you volunteer in the first place?"

To those overcommitters, I say, "Stay away!" You make our jobs more difficult by having us waste valuable time chasing you down. If other things come up that prevent you from fulfilling your commitments, just tell us. We'll understand. We can then move on, with no hard feelings.

Survival Tip:

For those of you who have had people fail to honor their commitment, here's what to do:

Give them two chances to get their act together:
1. Call them to get an explanation. Emergencies do happen. Last-minute work-related or family-related things happen.
2. Give them another date or assignment. Should they fail a second time, cut them loose. Volunteer them off the assignment or committee.

A lot of time and energy can be wasted chasing these people down. Let me tell you, you have other, more committed people available. Stick with them and move on.

Cell Phone Junkies

People Who Yak on Their Cellular Phones

I've had it with this new technology: cell phones. The industry has created a monster. People are talking all of the time, everywhere, and without consideration for others. Here's what is going on:

* Women using cell phones while they're in the bathroom on the toilet (men may be doing it as well).
* People holding conversations (often quite personal or professional) while on buses, trains, and airplanes.
* People standing in grocery store checkout lines, oblivious to the fact that their cart is on a collision course with the shopper in front of them. They hold everyone else up because, deep in conversation, they are not paying attention to what's going on.

* People making it a habit to have lengthy cell phone conversations while visiting you in *your* home.
* People at private functions, public functions, restaurants, and places of worship—you name it—they can't keep that cell phone out of their hands and away from their ears.
* And one last point. Cell phone junkies don't know how to whisper: the longer they talk, the louder they get. There ought to be a law against it.

Survival Tip:

This phenomenon is going to get worse before it gets better, so I say, "Prepare for the worst." Do your best to tune these people out. They are annoyances! Bring your Walkman along when traveling on public transportation. Sit as far away from these intrusive people as you can.

Should you be dining out, notify the manager if the noise becomes overwhelming. In some countries where cell phones are even more popular (can you imagine it?), there are restrictions on their use.

One last survival tip: Don't fight fire with fire by bringing your own phone to do battle! Gentle reader, you are better than that.☺

Chapter 3

Bathroom Things

Germ Carriers

People Who Don't Wash After Using the Bathroom

How can people think it's okay to use the bathroom and leave without washing their hands? Do you know the kinds of germs that can be spread? How disgusting!

I've seen it time and time again. Women walk right out of the stall and out the exit door. Men probably do it, too. With hands on the same door knob you'll have to use. Always remember to wash your hands. It takes just a little soap, water, and *voila!* Clean hands.

Survival Tip:

* If you shake hands regularly, you should carry anti-bacterial wipes. Though not a replacement for good old soap and water, in a crunch they're the next best thing. Doing so will take some of the fear out of shaking hands or touching things. Keep the wipes in your car, your office, your purse (women), and anywhere else you think a quick wipe might be necessary.
* If you have to exit the bathroom and are still a little shaky about opening the door, use a paper towel, a tissue, or one of those handy little handy wipes on the knob. It's just that simple. Remember, safety first!

Messy Wipers

People Who Splash Water on the Sink and Don't Wipe It Up

I know. I know. Using public washrooms can be disgusting. Even in the better restaurants and hotels you'll find that people refuse to wipe up behind themselves. I don't think I'm overreacting, but, folks, others follow you when you leave. Be considerate: let them arrive at a clean and water-free sink area. It takes only a few seconds to grab one paper towel and give it the old wipe-a-roo! It's called "bathroom manners."

Survival Tip:

* When you go into a restroom and there is water all over the sink, wipe the area you need to use. You'll feel more comfortable using the sink. I know it wasn't your mess, but rather than trying to avoid the water, it's easier to clean it up so you can put your purse (or men, whatever you are carrying) and other things on the counter.
* If you see a maintenance person, inform him or her that the bathroom needs servicing.
* If you're visiting someone's home, most definitely wipe the sink! Should you forget, people will know your messy little secret.

Naked Toilets

Companies That Don't Supply Toilet Seat Protectors

Equality still has a long way to go when it comes to the bathroom. This particular nerve worker is a woman's issue. I refuse to sit on a naked toilet seat. Although many women may not have as strong a concern about it, it is still a health issue. I am irritated by the fact that when I have to use the restroom, I must prepare the toilet seat before using it. You know: place toilet tissue on it before sitting down. What a lot of unnecessary work! If only there were seat covers available. I'd even settle for paper seat cover dispensers, though I prefer the automatic seat cover: just push the button, and you have a clean seat. None of that bending over, placing a sheet of toilet paper on either side of the toilet seat, and hoping the paper doesn't fall off before you're ready to sit down.

BEVERLY D. WASHINGTON

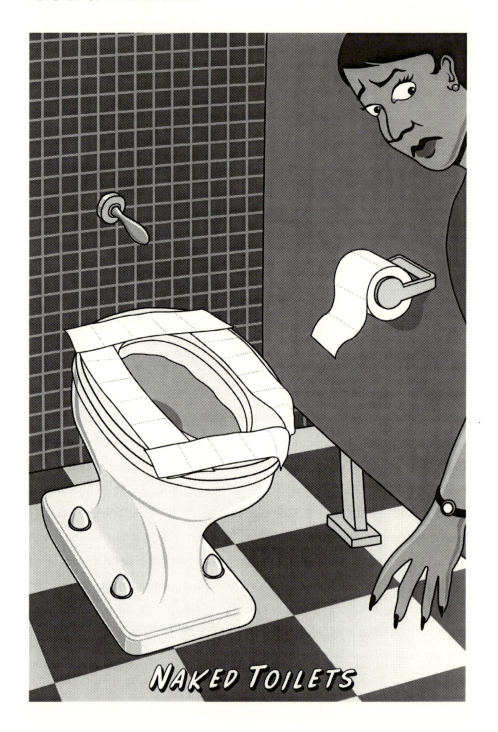

Survival Tip:

For the sake of convenience and consideration, companies should order automatic seat protectors so that women around the country can "push, pull down, and sit." Guys, we're only asking for a little speed and comfort. Isn't that what *you* have? Zip, pull, tuck, and go. And don't forget to wash those hands when you're done!☺

Chapter 4

Picking and Scratching Things

Grazers

People Who Eat from Open Bulk Food Containers

I'm surprised at the number of people who have a tendency to snatch a piece of fruit or a carrot from the produce section or salad bar and just keep on 'truckin'—especially if they decide to throw a few back in. What a disgusting thing! You don't know where their hands have been or if they've even washed them. What if you wanted to take a few items home or eat them for lunch? That fruit or vegetable may have already been touched several times. In the back of your mind, you're thinking, 'And *their hands*...Where have *they* been?' Beware of eating from open salad bars or bulk food areas. It can be hazardous to your health.

Survival Tip:

My best recommendation is:

* Avoid eating from open food bars and any other place where food is exposed to human hands.
* Stick with fruits that must be peeled before eating.
* Stick with packaged vegetables, but remember to wash them before eating.

Twirlers

People Who Play with Their Hair Around Open Food Bars

Because of what I've seen out there in grocery stores and restaurants, I automatically avoid little conveniences like open food bars because I've seen people do all sorts of things around them. When a person begins playing with her hair, there's the possibility that *anything* can fall out into exposed food.

Survival Tip:

As I mentioned in the previous survival tip, avoid open food bars as much as possible. They are unsanitary and can be unhealthy.

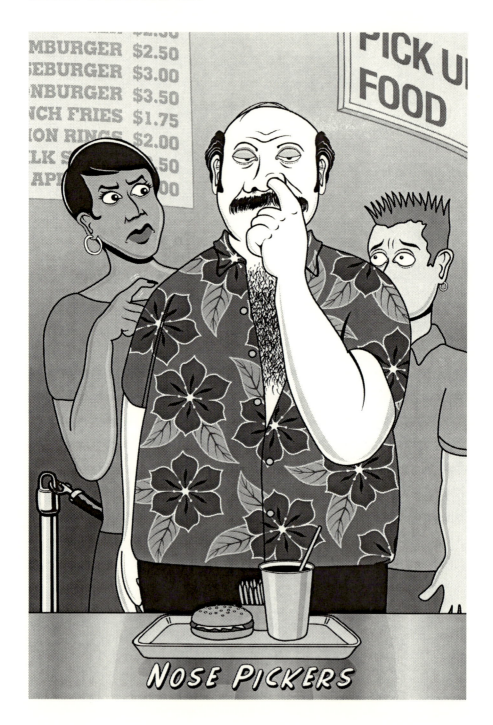

DON'T CALL ME "BEV"!

Nose Pickers

People Who Pick Their Nose in Public Places

I've always said, "Be careful what you do in public. Someone may be watching." You've seen it: people picking their nose in public. Ugly! There is that occasional itch or scratch to the outside of the nose. However, making a habit of actually picking your nose in public is so uncool and nauseating.

Survival Tip:

All I can say is for you to look away. Pickers will be pickers.☹

Privates Scratchers

Men Who Scratch Their Crotch in Public

Yes, I could have inserted this nerve worker earlier; however, I decided it warranted a place of its own.

Men, come on. It's revolting. You scratch. You readjust. You yank. You've even been caught doing such things on national television.

Do your readjusting in private—like in the bathroom before you have to exit. Take your time. Get it right. Then exit. Women all over the world will appreciate your consideration.

Survival Tip:

Ladies, if this crotch scratching happens in front of you, discreetly look away. Or, if you know the guy very well, remind him that there is a lady present. Or, better yet, embarrass the guy by asking him if he's finished.☺

Chapter 5

Food Things

Tongue Scoopers

People Who Use Their Tongue for Scooping Food

I know that when I sit down to eat with a person, I'm not supposed to be watching that person as he or she eats. I should, instead, be enjoying the person's company. Well, depending upon who the person might be, I can't always help observing his or her eating habits.

Have you ever observed a person's eating habits? Come on, be honest. I know that you have. You can tell a lot about people by their eating habits. People do the strangest things while eating.

One such thing is that they use their tongue to bring the food off the fork rather than putting the fork in their mouth. This is one of my nerve workers because I hate having to look at someone else's tongue move in and out of his mouth, scooping up food like a…um…I just can't bring myself to say it.

Survival Tip:

If you can, limit how often you eat out with that person. Need I say more?

Wide Mouths

People Who Talk with Their Mouth Full

I am aware that when dining out with others, spontaneous conversation happens. And most people who are considerate of others will at least chew and swallow as much of the food in their mouth as possible before talking. These people are not the ones I am referring to. I'm referring to those who eat and talk and smack with their mouth open with no consideration for others in their company. Either they lack manners or just don't care. Witnessing mashed-up food in someone's mouth is grotesque.

Survival Tip:

Should you eat out with someone who tends to talk with his or her mouth filled with food, refrain from asking any questions. Wait until the person has swallowed before continuing the conversation.

If you don't want to relive the unsightly experience, you may want to decline future dining invitations. It's just a thought.

Noisy Mouths

People Who Eat, Drink, and Smack on the Telephone

It's just plain rude to enjoy your meal in someone else's ear—or to blow out their eardrums by coughing in them, or to punish them as you suck down the phlegm from your sinuses to your throat. Gentle readers, people have sensibilities, too.

Survival Tip:

If someone calls you while they're eating, drinking, chewing, or smacking, cut your conversation with that person short. If you truly want to be helpful, inform him that you are having difficulty understanding him. The person may not be aware of his actions.

Gum Crackers

People Who Chew Gum Loudly and Pop It Incessantly

Age does have something to do with how poorly and inappropriately an individual should be allowed to behave. Children are still in training, since they're in the learning stages of life. However, adults of a certain age should know better than to exhibit certain behaviors in public.

When I was a child, it was okay to blow and "pop" our gum. It was a test of skill. As I said, I was much younger then.

Unfortunately, some adults have yet to grow out of such adolescent behavior. When gum poppers stand by me or sit near me, I quickly look for a way out. They get into a rhythm: pop, crack, pop. On and on and on. The more they enjoy the gum, the louder they get. Adults, you're in public. Mind your gum-chewing manners.

Survival Tip:

If you are near adult gum poppers, your only option is to move away...QUICKLY!☺

Ice Crunchers

People Who Chew Ice in Public

Here's another nerve worker that people should grow out of. How can a person think that no one can hear him chewing ice? Crunch, crunch, crunch, without regard for others. Chewing food can be noisy enough, but chewing ice? Why?

Survival Tip:

* If you find yourself sitting next to an ice chewer, you may have to bear with it for the short term, but move away if there is another place to go.
* Or, you can inform that person that his or her ice chewing can be heard and is distracting. The person will stop—maybe.

Teeth Suckers

People Who Suck Their Teeth After Eating

It is not uncommon to have food caught in between the teeth. The way it is removed, however, can be damaging to a person's image. The "thss, thss, thss" sound of someone trying to dislodge food from the crevices of a tooth is noisy! And annoying! Why is it that people think they can make these sounds without affecting someone?

Survival Tip:

If the person is a friend of yours, take him aside and explain to him that the noise that he is making is inappropriate and can be offensive to others. If the person is not a friend, give him this book as a gift with this page prominently marked.☺

Nose Blowers

People Who Use Dinner Napkins To Blow Their Nose

I've always thought that the dinner napkin was to be used to wipe (or dab) the corners of the mouth while eating. When will people get it right? The dinner napkin is for the MOUTH, NOT THE NOSE!

If blowing your nose is that serious, excuse yourself from the table and take care of any nose problems in the bathroom. If it's not a big problem, always carry tissues or a handkerchief for emergency blotting or light wiping of the nose. It's very difficult for others to enjoy their meal while someone is blowing his or her nose. Aaagh!

Survival Tip:

* If you noticed that the person used his napkin earlier to drain his nose, offer him one of your handy tissues, thwarting a second offense.

Should you not be comfortable with doing that, try the following:
- Focus your attention away from the nose blower *or*
- Bow your head and cough twice to help silence the noise *or*
- Strike up a conversation if you are seated next to someone.
- If none of the above suggestions work, close your eyes and hope that the blowing ends quickly and that the person doesn't use that part of the napkin to wipe his mouth.☺

Chapter 6

Street Things

BEVERLY D. WASHINGTON

Spitters

People Who Spit on Sidewalks

Expectorate. What a nice word to use instead of spit! Why must people spit on sidewalks, out of car windows, and wherever else they choose to? Big globs of saliva on the sidewalks. I make it a habit to watch where I walk.

I don't know about you, but I make a huge effort to protect the soles of my shoes. Others of you may not care, but I put stepping in spit right up there with stepping on bubble gum, in dog crap, or in vomit. I don't want someone's stuff stuck to the soles of my shoes. It's probably why I prefer that people remove their shoes before walking all over my carpet. I just can't afford to shampoo the carpet every day. If you're a spitter, please stop! It's disgusting! In some places there are laws against such behavior. Too bad these laws aren't adopted everywhere.

BEVERLY D. WASHINGTON

Survival Tip:

If you are like me and consider this a nerve worker, continue to watch where you walk. You never know what might be sticking to the soles of your shoes!

Blindsiders

People Who Don't Look Before Exiting a Room or Building

I'm walking down the sidewalk, and from out of nowhere, someone walks right into me. Would he or she ever think to look before entering a crowded sidewalk? Of course not! People are in their own little world. What's even worse is that oftentimes the person doesn't even bother to apologize. He or she bumps into you, nearly knocks you down, and then walks away without an apology.

Survival Tip:

If you are the person on the sidewalk, walk at least two feet away from an opening to a building or doorway—as someone exiting may not be paying attention and walk right into you. Be careful: it can be dangerous out there.☺

Weave Walkers

People Who Weave as They Walk Down the Street

While walking down the street, I am usually very careful to walk in a straight line, hugging at least one side of the sidewalk. This method of travel allows others to pass by should they choose to move at a faster pace. I seem to be in the minority, however. I find that some people think it is okay to weave from side to side as they walk down the street, paying absolutely no attention to the fact that others may want to pass. If you are a weaver, start paying attention! Stay to one side of the sidewalk. The same principles apply if you are driving a car. Well, perhaps not. Some drivers have difficulty staying in their lane. Anyway, think "one side" only.

Survival Tip:

If you happen to be walking behind a weaver, at the first opportunity to pass, do so. It may be several minutes before the next opportunity presents itself.

Hoggers

People Who Walk Shoulder to Shoulder on the Sidewalk

I enjoy having conversation with my friends as we walk down the street. The closer we are as we walk, the easier it is to hear each other's conversation. We also do our best to allow others to pass as we are walking. What bothers me is when other people walk two, three, or four people abreast, preventing others from getting by. Someone has to give. The sidewalk is not private property.

Survival Tip:

Should you find yourself having difficulty getting by people who monopolize the sidewalk, your only resort is to excuse yourself and break through.

Puffers

People Who Smoke in Front of Building Entrances

All day long, working professionals go in and out of office buildings. Oftentimes, they have a difficult time maneuvering because of smokers who stand outside the entrances puffing on cigarettes. I spend quite a bit of time grooming myself for the business day only to, in many cases, encounter a smoker blowing smoke right in my pathway. Though a nonsmoker, I do not have anything against smokers, but I would appreciate not being subjected to their fumes. After all, who wants to smell like cigarette smoke when going in to meet a client?

Survival Tip:

Time your entrances and exits. This may be your only recourse. If there is another doorway available, *run*—don't walk—to avoid the puffs of a smoker.

Roadblockers

People Who Stand in the Middle of Corridors and Aisles

I was taught to stand to one side of a corridor so others can get by. Was I the only one taught this lesson? It amazes me that people stand in the middle of an aisle or hallway, preventing others from passing. This always happens to me when I'm in a hurry. I've even witnessed this rude behavior on escalators and on (airport) moving walkways where the sign clearly reads "Stand right, Walk left." Offenders should remember that, one day, they might be in a hurry and need the favor returned.

Survival Tip:

If you seem to be encountering these middle-of-the-roaders, avoid walking between them. Politely excuse yourself and walk through, or you can announce, "On your left, please." It's a signal that bikers and skaters yell as they pass by. It works for them; perhaps it will work for you.

Chapter 7

Surprise Things

DON'T CALL ME "BEV"!

Clueless

People Who Give Thoughtless Gifts

When I give gifts, I make it a practice to give nice ones. I also spend time thinking about the person, making the gift meaningful and perhaps practical. A gift should be given from the heart with the appearance that some investment of time and consideration have been made. Unfortunately, not everyone is as thoughtful. If you can't choose your gifts with care and thought, then refrain from giving a gift at all. Instead, buy a nice card (valued at least three dollars). Or, you can come up with your own creative way to show the person that you appreciate him or her.

Survival Tip:

If you are on the receiving end of what appears to be a thoughtless gift, say, "Thank you." Show your good manners.☺

Cheap Tippers

People Who Don't Tip Appropriately

Figuring out a gratuity can be challenging if your math isn't quite up to snuff. Is it 15 percent or 20 percent? If you stay somewhere close to these percentages, you'll be okay, but there are those people who are just plain CHEAP. They don't tip at all, as if they think that leaving a gratuity would break the bank. If you've had a great meal and the waitstaff performed excellently, do the right thing: leave the gratuity. How embarrassing not to leave a tip at all or to leave an inappropriate tip and allow your eating companions to discover your cheapness! See if they dine with you again!

Survival Tip:

If you have difficulty figuring out the gratuity, use the 10-percent rule times two. If worse comes to worse, carry a tip card with you. When the check arrives, excuse yourself momentarily, and go to the restroom and check the card. You'll never go wrong. Return to the table, confident that you'll do the right thing.

Surprisers

People Who Bring Uninvited Guests to a Party

You've counted, recounted, and confirmed the number of guests you've invited to your party. The invitations have been sent. You have enough food. You've made out the seating assignments, and all is well. Well, not quite. You now have to make room for uninvited guests: the invitees neglected to inform you that they were bringing a few others.

Now, I don't mind friends of friends coming to my parties. However, it would be nice to be informed in advance.

Survival Tip:

Should this discourtesy happen to you, and the uninvited guests are at your door, smile and treat them as you would any invited guest. If they turn out to be great people, get their names and numbers and add them to your mailing list for future invites. Should they not, don't bother. By all means, inform the guest who extended the invitation that you would appreciate a heads-up in the future.

Cheapskates

People Who Don't Pay Their Fair Share When Dining Out

I don't mind going out to dinner with friends. In fact, I enjoy the company of others when dining. I have some issues, however, with those who eat more (or more expensively) than what they are willing to pay for. Even worse is dining with a person who is always attempting to shortchange you. I have had enough with these "el cheapoes"!

Survival Tip:

Everyone is responsible for his or her share of the bill. If you are put in the same position, I suggest asking the waitstaff for separate checks when only two diners are involved. This avoids having to do calculations at the table. When dining out with many others, split the bill equally, pay it, and be on your way.

Slim Stickers

People Who Drink with the Stirrer Still in the Glass

I've never understood why people don't remove the stirrers from their drinks after they have mixed the beverage. It's amusing to watch them drink their beverage while trying to avoid poking themselves in the face with the stirrer—or, even worse, watching them try to sip through the stirrer. Stirrers are not straws, so they should be removed.

Survival Tip:

Humorously, you can suggest that they remove the stirrer from their beverage for safety's sake. If they refuse, just don't be seen in public with that person again.☺

Chapter 8

Retail Sales Things

Chit-Chatters

Salespeople Who Socialize with Others While Waiting on You

It's annoying to have to overhear a salesperson's personal conversation as he or she takes care of a customer's transaction. This problem occurs everywhere: at the post office, grocery store, department stores—you name it. I can't take all the chatter. Employees have breaks for that. They should save the socializing until then.

Another reason this problem is so unnerving is that it slows up the transaction, taking the clerk more time to complete the task. I want to get in and out, so please stop the chatter!

Survival Tip:

Should you find yourself in a position in which a clerk is more interested in tending to his or her social life than to your transaction, politely ask the person to complete the transaction before continuing on. And if he or she is disturbed by the request, direct your concerns to the manager. That should get you results. Or, you can always get satisfaction by spending your money elsewhere.

Unprofessionals

Salespeople Who Argue with Their Customers

I know that the customer isn't *always* right, but the customer is still the customer. And professional salespeople are responsible for rising above any urge to argue with customers.

I remember early in my professional career getting into an argument with a customer. He was truly in error; however, he was the customer. Nevertheless, I had to prove my point. Let me tell you: it was an awful experience, and I swore that I would never do it again. Salespeople, take my advice: it is not worth the trouble to argue with customers. Besides, it's unprofessional.

Survival Tip:

If you are ever faced with a salesperson who wants to argue with you about an issue, *don't*. Remain calm and point out the facts as you know them. Should that not work, immediately ask to speak with the manager. Dealing with an argumentative salesperson will only stress you out. It's not worth it!

Chapter 9

Movie Things

Story Blockers

People Who Want To Tell You the Plot of a Movie

I enjoy going to the movies, although I seldom do these days. When I do, however, I am very selective about the people I accompany. I remember going out to a movie with a guy I once dated. (It was the first and last time we went to a movie.) For some reason, he felt the need to talk to me about the plot, and he talked at the screen throughout the movie. Movie manners were not high on his list of priorities.

Survival Tip:

If you find yourself in a similar predicament, inform your companion that the movie is one that you have read a lot about and that you want to concentrate on every scene. Just hope that person gets the hint. If not, never go to the movie with that person again.

Interrupters

People Who Talk During Films

Movie Etiquette 101: Before the start of a movie, it's okay to have casual conversation, but when the movie begins, all conversation should cease. Still, most people don't get it. They talk and talk and talk. It's as though they come to the theatre to discuss the day's events. And no number of stares from people or shushing will stop them. So what to do next?

Survival Tip:

* Find another seat.
* Ask the movie attendant to intervene.
* Leave and ask for your money back. Then return during a quieter time. The management will usually oblige.

Reactors

People Who Talk at the Movie Screen

I'm sure that during a movie, you, too, have blurted out an instruction or two to the actors during an *intense* moment. Yes, you no doubt have. And so have I. During an exciting or frightening moment, you yelled something at the movie screen and afterwards may have slipped down into your seat with embarrassment.

We've all gotten a bit emotional at a movie at one time or another, but what about those people who constantly talk and yell and give instructions to the actors on the screen. The actors can't hear you. It's only a movie. So what can a person do?

Survival Tip:

* Suggestion 1: Be selective about where you venture out to see your favorite flick. There are movie houses where people don't practice movie etiquette. Cross them off your list.
* Suggestion 2: Go during less popular times of the day or week. Weekday matinees might be a good bet.
* Suggestion 3: Wait for the video to come out. You can then enjoy the movie in the comfort and privacy of your own home with no distractions.☺

Chapter 10

Travel Things

Aisle Hoggers

People Who Pull Oversized Luggage Down Airplane Aisles

People are funny, and many don't know just how funny they can be. It happens at least once on every flight I take: someone can't get his or her luggage cart down the aisle. Often, the cart is too wide to be carried on board in the first place—and instead of pushing down the handle and carrying the cart, he or she unsuccessfully continues to pull it, delaying the people behind.

Survival Tip:

If you are the one affected by the delay, you might politely suggest that he or she pick up the cart and carry it down the narrow aisle. The offender might get a little ticked off, so at the end of your suggestion, throw a warm smile to smooth things over.☺

Space Stealers

People Who Put Their Luggage Underneath Their Seats

Hello, person in the bulkhead seat. Your luggage belongs in the overhead compartment, not under *your* seat, which happens to be the space for *my* carry-on, legs, and feet.

It is amazing to me to still find air travelers who do not know the rules of air travel. It is, and has always been, that the person seated in the bulkhead must store his carry-on in the overhead. But, as you know, there are travelers who continue to bring on board more than their fair share of luggage and want to occupy more than their fair share of storage space. Bulkhead sitters, reach for the overhead. *REACH FOR THE OVERHEAD!*

Survival Tip:

If the person in front of you tries to take over your leg room, suggest to him that your luggage already occupies the space under his seat. Propose, with a smile, that he call the flight attendant for help in relocating his luggage.

Seat Tuggers

People Who Tug and Lean on Your Seatback

Whoever said that my seatback is to be used to brace you when you're trying to get in and out of your seat?

Every time I'm comfortably seated in my seat, someone presses on it to get up—and presses on it again to sit back down. On longer flights, people stand in the aisles having conversations with someone in the seat behind mine, *and* they insist on leaning on my seat. Air travelers, it's Airplane Etiquette 101: Press on your own seat to enter and exit your space.

Survival Tip:

* When this happens to you, ask, moderately loudly, "What's happening? What's going on?" Then turn around to the person behind you, and give him a puzzled look. The person should get the message and apologize. He or she will likely be more careful upon returning.
* Request a window seat when booking your flight. Offenders usually press on the middle and aisle seats. You're safer with a window seat. Every little trick helps.☺

Chapter 11

Hotel Things

BEVERLY D. WASHINGTON

Room Doom

Hotel Rooms That Have Not Been Properly Cleaned

What an awful thought: walking into a hotel room that has not been properly cleaned! What has happened to quality control?

Room doom has happened to me only a few times, and one of the times the hotel was undergoing construction. Still, it's no excuse.

Survival Tip:

Before unpacking your luggage, inspect the room carefully. Start with the bathroom; next, pull the bedspread back to check the sheets. Lastly, take time to inspect the carpet. If anything is out of order, hurry down to the check-in desk and ask for another room. If another room is not available, ask the desk clerk to inspect the room with you, and suggest a discount on the room and a new set of clean linen. You'll feel some comfort. In a worst-case scenario, have the hotel desk clerk locate another hotel for you—of course, at their expense.

Half-Views

Hotels That Lack Full-length Mirrors in the Guest Rooms

When traveling on business, I always need to consult a full-length mirror before leaving my room. I want to look my best when meeting a client and while on vacation, but I have found that many hotel chains do not install full-length mirrors, a necessity for proper grooming. Is there a shortage, or are the hotels being cheap? Probably just cheap!

Survival Tip:

Before confirming a room, inquire whether the hotel has full-length mirrors and the other essentials such as an iron, ironing board, shampoo, and lotion. If the answer is no, book another hotel. It's just that simple.

Inconsiderates

Guests Who Carry on Loud Conversations in the Hallways

I'm on vacation and trying to relax in bed, getting that last bit of shut-eye, when all of a sudden I overhear loud conversations coming from the hallway. A guest of the hotel is out in the hallway talking as loudly as he can, as if he were out in a ballpark. I'm unable to sleep or even relax. It's unfair. Guests should be considerate of others.

Survival Tip:

If the chatter continues, politely suggest to the offender that he may want to continue the conversation in his room. Should that not work, call the front desk and inform management as to what is happening on your floor. Ask that they send someone up to handle the matter.

Chapter 12

Other Things

BEVERLY D. WASHINGTON

Advantage Takers

People Who Try To Take Advantage of You

I had a client who attempted to take unfair advantage of me. This person kept putting me off about a project I'd worked on. The audacity! Fortunately, I did have a signed contract, and he had to pay. Yes, he had to pay.

Beware! There are people out there who, for whatever reason, will try to take advantage of you. The offense could be as minor as forgetting to return something borrowed to something as major as reneging on an agreement. It's a fact of life.

Survival Tip:

When the offense has to do with a financial deal, always have the person sign a contract. Require that they also pay a deposit. Proceed with caution should you decide to continue doing business with that company or individual.

If the offense happens to be with an associate or even a friend, it may be time to sit down and have a heart-to-heart talk. Point out your concerns. Should the person not take your concerns seriously, you may need to reevaluate the relationship.

Insinceres

People Who Don't Keep Their Word

A person gives you his word. He sounds sincere. You continue to take him at his word. Then, lo and behold, he lets you down by not keeping his word.

It's about integrity. It's about your reputation. Your word is who you are. *Don't blow it!*

BEVERLY D. WASHINGTON

Survival Tip:

Business:
* Always get everything in writing.
* Have everything signed.
* Keep your attorney, if you have one, involved.
* If you don't have an attorney, hire one. It's the only way that you will be taken seriously.

Personal:
* Evaluate your friends carefully.
* Observe what a person says and does. If there are any inconsistencies...RUN! You don't want to be that person's next victim.☹

Excuse Makers

People Who Make Excuses for Anything and Everything

You meet a person, and he or she seems to be nice enough. But after being around the person a bit more, you hear in his conversation that nothing is going right for him. You, being an optimist, suggest things that have worked for you. The person rejects your advice and continues to complain, moan, and groan about life being unfair.

Gentle readers, pay attention to what you are hearing from these people before you get sucked into their negativity. If this person says that nothing ever goes right for him and blames his problems on everyone else...FIND THE CLOSEST EXIT!

Survival Tip:

Stay away from negative people. Stay away from people who are not willing to take responsibility for their lives. Stay away from people who are not willing to change things for the better.

As adults, we must take responsibility for our lives. Yes, there may be things that are not within our control, but after we recognize what these things are, it is up to us to take action. Taking action could be changing where you live, updating your skills, or eliminating toxic people from your life. The bottom line is that you must take action to get your life moving in the right direction. Remember: It's not that life isn't fair; life is life. Live it with a positive attitude.

Sincerely,

Beverly, not *Bev*!

About the Author

Beverly Washington is a successful entrepreneur, motivational speaker, model, and television host. She divides her time and talents among traveling nationally and internationally; conducting effectiveness training seminars for corporations; and producing and hosting a cable television show on personal empowerment, *Stop the Drama*—all under the company she founded: IMAGE FACTOR, INC.

Beverly has expanded her talents to include acting. She has appeared in television commercials and print ads for such well-known brands as Sears, JC Penney, Kraft, McDonald's, Motorola, Hallmark Cards, and Kellogg's.

With a bachelor of fine arts degree in dance education from the University of Illinois, Urbana-Champaign, Beverly was also an All-American high jumper and long jumper and member of the Midwest All-American track and field team participating in the 1979 U.S. Olympic Training Camp in Colorado Springs.

CPSIA information can be obtained at www.ICGtesting.com
Printed in the USA
LVOW040448301112

309300LV00003B/172/A